D1518948

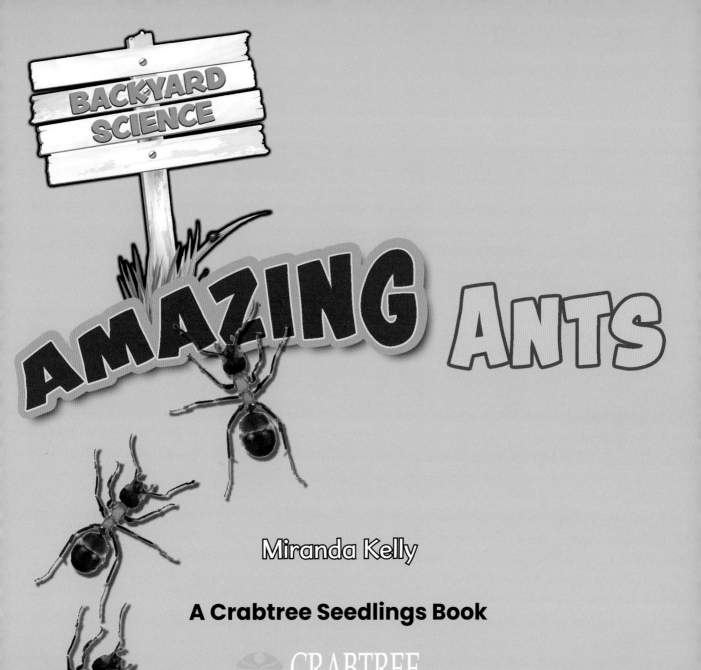

BACKYARD SCIENCE

AMAZING ANTS

Miranda Kelly

A Crabtree Seedlings Book

CRABTREE
Publishing Company
www.crabtreebooks.com

TABLE OF CONTENTS

Ants

You might think ants are creepy, crawly pests. But the people who study them think they are the most interesting **insects** on Earth.

Ants live and work together in a **colony**. Colonies can range from about 50 ants to millions of ants.

Most colonies have three kinds of ants: at least one egg-laying **queen**, other female ants, and males.

queen ant

queen
(KWEEN)

Ant Jobs

Every ant has a job in the colony.
The queen's job is to lay eggs.
She keeps the colony growing.

Male ants are called **drones**. They mate with future queens. Drones often fly away to find a new colony and queen.

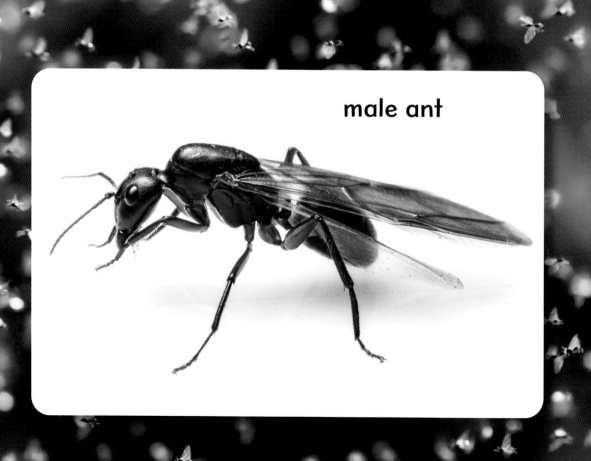
male ant

drone
(DROHN)

13

female worker ant

Worker ants are female. They protect the queen, **forage** for food, and care for the nest.

Ant Nests

All ant nests are different. Ants build nests that work with the **environment**.

18

Ant Raids

In order to feed the colony, ants forage in large groups called raids.

Some ant colonies will eat thousands of insects a day.

Glossary

colony (KOL-uh-nee): A colony is a large group of animals that live together, such as a colony of ants.

drones (DROHNZ): Drones are male ants whose job is to mate with the queen.

environment (en-VYE-ruhn-muhnt): The environment is the natural world of Earth's air, land, and water.

forage (FOR-ij): To forage is to search for food.

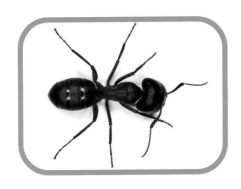

insects (IN-sekts): Insects are small animals with six legs, three body sections, and no backbone.

queen (KWEEN): The queen is the one female ant whose job is to lay eggs.

Index

23

School-to-Home Support for Caregivers and Teachers

This book helps children grow by letting them practice reading. Here are a few guiding questions to help the reader build his or her comprehension skills. Possible answers appear here in red.

Before Reading

- **What do I think this book is about?** I think this book is about the many unique things that ants do. I think this book is about how and where ants live.

- **What do I want to learn about this topic?** I want to learn more about why some ants sting people. I want to learn how ants can move objects that are so much larger than themselves.

During Reading

- **I wonder why...** I wonder why ants live in large groups. I wonder why male ants are called drones.

- **What have I learned so far?** I have learned that ants have at least one egg-laying queen in each colony. I have learned that an ant colony can have 50 ants to millions of ants.

After Reading

- **What details did I learn about this topic?** I have learned that the worker ants are females. I have learned that the worker ants protect the queen, forage for food, and care for the nest.

- **Read the book again and look for the glossary words.** I see the word *colony* on page 6, and the word *forage* on page 15. The other glossary words are found on pages 22 and 23.

Library and Archives Canada Cataloguing in Publication

CIP available at Library and Archives Canada

Library of Congress Cataloging-in-Publication Data

CIP available at Library of Congress

Crabtree Publishing Company

www.crabtreebooks.com   1–800–387–7650

Print book version produced jointly with Blue Door Education in 2022

Written by: Miranda Kelly

Production coordinator and Prepress technician: Tammy McGarr

Print coordinator: Katherine Berti

Printed in the U.S.A./CG20210915/012022

PHOTO CREDITS:
Istock.com, shutterstock.com, Cover: ConstantinCornel. Pg2/3; PhanuwatNandee. Pg4/5: Credit:Anterovium. Pg6/7: fotoco-istock. Pg8/9; markhonosvitaly, akwitps. Pg10/11; Pavel Krasensky. Pg12/13; Digoarpi, Jamraslamyai | Dreamstime.com. Pg14/15; webguzs, Iamyai. Pg16/17; Mark R Coons, Ignatiev, cweimer4. Pg18/19; thatreec, verapon. Pg20/21; popphoto2526, Poravute. Pg22/23; mypicksy, Maor Winetrob, Henrik_L, Pavel Krasensky, andreasgaertner, © Jamraslamyai | Dreamstime.com.

Published in the United States
Crabtree Publishing
347 Fifth Ave.
Suite 1402-145
New York, NY 10016

Published in Canada
Crabtree Publishing
616 Welland Ave.
St. Catharines, Ontario
L2M 5V6